GW00706070

This book belongs to

LYNN YOUNG

A Book of Wit and Wisdom

HAPPY 40th BIRTHDAY

Edited by Julie Mars

Ariel Books

Andrews and McMeel
Kansas City

H A P P Y   4 0 t h   B I R T H D A Y

FRONTISPIECE BY JUDITH A. STAGNITTO

ISBN: 0-8362-3095-7
Library of Congress Catalog Card Number: 94-71128

HAPPY 40th BIRTHDAY

Introduction

Let's face it: It happens to everyone—*the Big Four-Oh.* Whether we welcome the change or dread it, whether we view it as a milestone of achievement or a millstone pulling us down into middle age, we can't ignore the often not-so-subtle sting of the fortieth birthday.

But don't despair! The forties don't have to be frightening. Lots of folks shine like gold after forty. Think of George Washington—he led a revolution at age forty-three. Or Christopher Columbus—he set out to find the New World at forty-one. Or Britain's Edward VIII: Completely in love, he abdicated at age forty-three to marry the American divorcée Wallis Simpson.

Maybe youth *is* ending . . . but something new and different is just beginning. And after all, as the old line goes, today is the first day of the rest of your life!

Age is strictly a case of mind over matter. If you don't mind, it doesn't matter.

— *Jack Benny*

When women pass thirty, they first forget their age; when forty, they forget that they ever remembered it.

— *Ninon de L'Enclos*

Middle age: when you're sitting at home on Saturday night and the telephone rings and you hope it isn't for you.

— *Ogden Nash*

My forties are the best time I have ever gone through.

— *Elizabeth Taylor*

At middle age the soul should be opening up like a rose, not closing up like a cabbage.

— *John Andrew Holmes*

Youth lacks, to some extent, experience.

— *Spiro T. Agnew*

Just remember, once you're over the hill you begin to pick up speed.

Charles M. Schulz

One of the many things nobody ever tells you about middle age is that it's such a nice change from being young.

— *Dorothy Canfield Fisher*

Age, we find, is a time for hurry to get a lot of things done that youth should have accomplished but postponed doing.

— *Franklin P. Adams*

After thirty, a body has a mind of its own.

—*Bette Midler*

I've always felt proud of my age. I think people should be proud that they've been around long enough to have learned something.

—*Frances Moore Lappé*

The five B's of middle age—bald-ness, bridgework, bifocals, bay windows, and bunions.

— *Anonymous*

It may be true that *life* begins at forty, but everything else starts to wear out, fall out, or spread out.

—*Beryl Pfizer*

To hold the same views at forty as we held at twenty is to have been stupefied for a score of years, and take rank, not as a prophet, but as an unteachable brat, well birched and none the wiser.

— *Robert Louis Stevenson*

Middle age is when you're faced with two temptations and you choose the one that will get you home by nine o'clock.

— *Ronald Reagan*

Perhaps middle age is, or should be, a period of shedding shells; the shell of ambition, the shell of material accumulations and possessions, the shell of the ego.

— *Anne Morrow Lindbergh*

Middle age is when your age starts to show around your middle.

— *Bob Hope*

20

We don't understand life any better at forty than at twenty, but we know it and admit it.

—*Jules Renard*

We grow neither better nor worse as we get old, but more like ourselves.

—*May Lamberton Becker*

You grow up the day you have your first real laugh—at yourself.

— *Ethel Barrymore*

Age gives good advice when it is no longer able to give a bad example.

— *American proverb*

. . . The only thing really wrong with turning forty is that we can't do it while we're still twenty-five.

—*Janet Scott Barlow*

Middle age: when you begin to exchange your emotions for symptoms.

—*Irvin S. Cobb*

I'm at the age where food has taken the place of sex in my life. In fact, I've just had a mirror put over my kitchen table.

—*Rodney Dangerfield*

The old believe in everything; the middle-aged suspect everything; the young know everything.

—*Oscar Wilde*

We are always the same age inside.

— *Gertrude Stein*

At the age of forty . . . her fire may be covered with ashes, but it is not extinguished.

— *Mary Wortley Montagu*

The first forty years of life give us the text; the next thirty supply the commentary.

— *Arthur Schopenhauer*

Any man worth his salt has by the time he is forty-five accumulated a crown of thorns, and the problem is to learn to wear it over one ear.

— *Christopher Morley*

At thirty, man suspects himself a
    fool;
Knows it at forty, and reforms his
    plan. . .

— *Edward Young*

Every man over forty is a
scoundrel.

— *George Bernard Shaw*

Middle age is when a man figures he has enough financial security to wear the flashy sports coats he didn't have the courage to wear when he was young.

—*Bill Vaughan*

At sixteen I was stupid, confused, insecure and indecisive. At twenty-five I was wise, self-confident, pre-possessing and assertive. At forty-five, I am stupid, confused, insecure and indecisive. Who would have supposed that maturity is only a short break in adolescence?

—*Jules Feiffer*

Age is a very high price to pay for maturity.

—*Tom Stoppard*

Whoever is not a misanthrope at forty can never have loved mankind.

—*Nicolas Chamfort*

A man of forty today has nothing to worry him but falling hair, inability to button the top button, failing vision, shortness of breath, a tendency of the collar to shut off all breathing, trembling of the kidneys to whatever tune the orchestra is playing, and a general sense of giddiness when the matter of rent is brought up. Forty is Life's Golden Age.

—Robert Benchley

Middle Age—Later than you think and sooner than you expect.

—*Earl Wilson*

He that is not handsome at twenty, nor strong at thirty, nor rich at forty, nor wise at fifty, will never be handsome, strong, rich, or wise.

—*George Herbert*

Anybody can get old. All you have to do is go on living.

— *Groucho Marx*

Forty is the old age of youth; fifty is the youth of old age.

— *French proverb*

As for books like *Life Begins at Forty,* they're comforting to read, but they're about as close to the truth as near beer.

—*Jane Goodsell*

To divide one's life by years is of course to tumble into a trap set by our own arithmetic.

—*Clifton Fadiman*

34

What is an adult? A child blown up by age.

— *Simone de Beauvoir*

Youth is the time of getting, middle age of improving, and old age of spending.

— *Anne Bradstreet*

I am just turning forty and taking my time about it.

—*Harold Lloyd (at 77)*

Forty and forty-five are bad enough; fifty is simply hell to face; fifteen minutes after that you are sixty; and then in ten minutes more you are eighty-five.

—*Don Marquis*

Life begins at forty.

—Sophie Tucker

The really frightening thing about middle age is the knowledge that you'll grow out of it.

—Doris Day

Women begin to hit their stride in their forties. . . .

— *Cokie Roberts*

Middle-aged life is merry, and I love to lead it.

— *Ogden Nash*

The youth gets together his materials to build a bridge to the moon . . . and, at length, the middle-aged man concludes to build a woodshed with them.

—Henry David Thoreau

At eighteen, one adores at once; at twenty, one loves; at thirty, one desires; at forty, one reflects.

—*Paul de Kock*

[Middle age is] when a man is warned to slow down by a doctor instead of a policeman.

—*Sidney Brody*

One of the signs of passing youth is the birth of a sense of fellowship with other human beings as we take our place among them.

—*Virginia Woolf*

Middle age occurs when you are too young to take up golf and too old to rush up to the net.

— *Franklin P. Adams*

Forty years on, growing older and
   older,
Shorter in wind, as in memory long,
Feeble of foot, and rheumatic of
   shoulder
What will it help you that once you
   were strong?

—E. E. Bowen

A woman past forty should make up her *mind* to be young, not her face.

—Billie Burke

44

When we get to be forty or forty-five years old we have a wonderful base of experience to transform ourselves. It takes incredible courage to leap off the bridge of what we've known, who we've been, and how we've defined ourselves, but there's so much richness in the water below when we jump.

—*Brooke Medicine Eagle*

One of the pleasures of middle age is to *find out* that one WAS right, and that one was much righter than one knew at say seventeen or twenty-three.

— *Ezra Pound*

Youth supplies us with colors, age with canvas.

— *Henry David Thoreau*

Women are as beautiful as flowers when they are forty years old.

—— *Chinese proverb*

Age is nothing but a number. It is how you use it.

— *Ethel Payne*

Middle age is when your old classmates are so grey and wrinkled and bald they don't recognize you.

— *Bennett Cerf*

Forty times over let Michaelmas
  pass,
Grizzling hair the brain doth clear—
Then you know a boy is an ass,
Then you know the worth of a lass,
  Once you have come to forty year.

—W. M. Thackeray

Midway between youth and age like a man who has missed his train: too late for the last and too early for the next.

—*George Bernard Shaw*

Men have as many years as they feel, women as many as they show.

—*Italian proverb*

Perhaps one can at last in middle age, if not earlier, be completely oneself. And what a liberation that would be.

—*Anne Morrow Lindbergh*

Of all the barbarous middle ages,
    that
Which is the most barbarous is the
    middle age
Of man; it is—I really scarce know
    what;
But when we hover between fool
    and sage.

—*Lord Byron*

It is sad to grow old but nice to ripen.

—*Brigitte Bardot*

At twenty years of age the will reigns; at thirty the wit; at forty the judgment.

—*Benjamin Franklin*

There is a fountain of youth: it is your mind, your talents, the creativity you bring to your life and the lives of people you love. When you learn to tap this source, you will have truly defeated age.

—Sophia Loren

We do not have a childhood, a maturity, an old age: several times during our lives we have our seasons, but their course is not well known: it is not clearly laid out.

—*Jules Renard*

With steady foot and even pace
I tread the Milky Way;
I've youth without its levity
And age without decay.

—*Daniel Defoe*

Age is only a number, a cipher for the records. A man can't retire his experience. He must use it. Experience achieves more with less energy and time.

— *Bernard Baruch*

Each age, like every individual, has its own characteristic intoxication. . . .

— *Will Durant*

56

On passing his fortieth year, any man of the slightest power of mind . . . will hardly fail to show some trace of misanthropy.

—*Arthur Schopenhauer*

At forty I attained to an unperturbed mind.

—*Mencius*

Rashness is the error of youth, timid caution of age. Manhood is . . . the ripe and fertile season of action, when alone we can hope to find the head to contrive, united with the hand to execute.

— *Charles Caleb Colton*

In a man's middle years there is scarcely a part of the body he would hesitate to turn over to the proper authorities.

— *E. B. White*

No spring, nor summer beauty hath such grace,
As I have seen in one autumnal face.

— *John Donne*

As we grow old . . . the beauty steals inward.

—*Ralph Waldo Emerson*

I love everything that's old: old friends, old times, old manners, old books, old wines.

—*Oliver Goldsmith*

By the time we've made it, we've had it.

—*Malcolm Forbes*

For age is opportunity no less
Than youth itself, though in another
   dress,
And as the evening twilight fades
   away
The sky is filled with stars, invisible
   by day.

— *Henry Wadsworth*
   Longfellow

We turn not older with years, but newer every day.

—*Emily Dickinson*

Better one bite, at forty, of Truth's
  bitter rind
Than the hot wine that gushed from
  the vintage of twenty!

—*James Russell Lowell*

I have no romantic feelings about age. Either you are interesting at any age or you are not. There is nothing particularly interesting about being old—or being young, for that matter.

— *Katharine Hepburn*

It is unjust to claim the privileges of age, and retain the playthings of childhood.

— *Samuel Johnson*

I look forward to growing old and wise and audacious.

— *Glenda Jackson*

The old woman I will become will be quite different from the woman I am now. Another "I" is beginning, and so far I have not had to complain of her.

— *George Sand*

Paradoxical as it may seem, to believe in youth is to look backward; to look forward we must believe in age.

—*Dorothy L. Sayers*

How unnatural the imposed view, imposed by a puritanical ethos, that passionate love belongs only to the young, that people are dead from the neck down by the time they are forty, and that any deep feeling, any passion after that age, is either ludicrous or revolting!

—*May Sarton*

I've always roared with laughter when they say life begins at forty. That's the funniest remark ever. The day I was born was when life began for me.

—*Bette Davis*

I grow more intense as I age.

—*Florida Scott-Maxwell*

You Know You're Over Forty When...

- your "loose" jeans are getting too tight.

- you know your cholesterol count by heart.

- all your friends wear bifocals.

- you look at your watch and see your biological clock ticking.

- you express your adventurous streak by skipping your basket-weaving class.

- your center of gravity is at an all-time low.

- it takes you longer to get into your running outfit than it does to do your evening jog.

- it's a crisis when you can't find the remote control device.

- your kids refer to your youth as the "olden days."

- a night out with friends ends at nine o'clock.

- your college record collection is suddenly valuable.

- you can't remember why you dreaded turning thirty.

- you go to your class reunion and everybody does the twist.

• you convince yourself that you're not coloring your hair . . . you're working with it.

• your kids finally grow up and don't move out.

• you check into a motel with your spouse and your first thought is if there's enough room on the bathroom counter to line up your prescriptions.

• the summer heat waves are

mild in comparison to your hot flashes.

- most of your belts have suddenly shrunk.

- you think you need more than one pair of control-top panty hose.

- you've been up after midnight only three times in the past year.

- you find yourself seriously studying advertisements about hair transplants.

• your treadmill test is more exercise than you've had in three months.

• your son comes home with a pierced nose and you nostalgically wish he'd done his ear instead.

Fortieth Birthday Gifts You Should Never Give:

MEN

- a blood pressure monitor

- a "Sex After Forty" training manual

- clippers for nose and ear hairs

- membership in the local shuffle-board club

• a scholarly textbook on preparing for the inevitable mid-life crisis

WOMEN

- a bottle of Geritol

- super-strength support hose

- any book on "Living with Menopause"

- an undershirt

- an in-depth study of the "Empty Nest Syndrome"

Strangest New Experiences

- being called ma'am or sir

- your very first white eyebrow hair

- the first time a stranger is not surprised to learn your grown children are your children

- watching a hot, romantic movie and not being able to figure out what the fuss is all about

- your parents actually listening to your opinions on something

- finding yourself warning your daughter about guys who are exactly like you used to be

- someone telling you, you look fantastic *for your age*

This text of this book was set in
Stempel Schneidler and the display
in Kaufmann, using Quark Xpress
and Adobe Illustrator.

Book design, illustrations, and
typesetting by

JUDITH A. STAGNITTO